Usborne

First Sticker Book

SPACE

Contents

Illustrated by Alistar

Words by Sam Smith
Designed by Sharon Cooper

Out in space

Our planet, the Earth, is one of eight planets that go around the Sun. Stick all the planets onto the picture, then add some asteroids and comets whizzing through space.

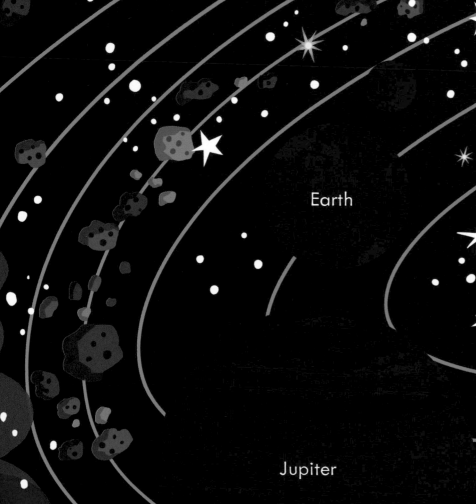

Uranus

Sun

Earth

Mercury

Jupiter

Neptune

Mars

Venus

Saturn

3

Exploring space

More than 50 years ago, machines called satellites were first sent into space to find out more about it. Soon afterwards, people called astronauts went up into space in rockets. Use the stickers to fill these pages with lots of different rockets and satellites.

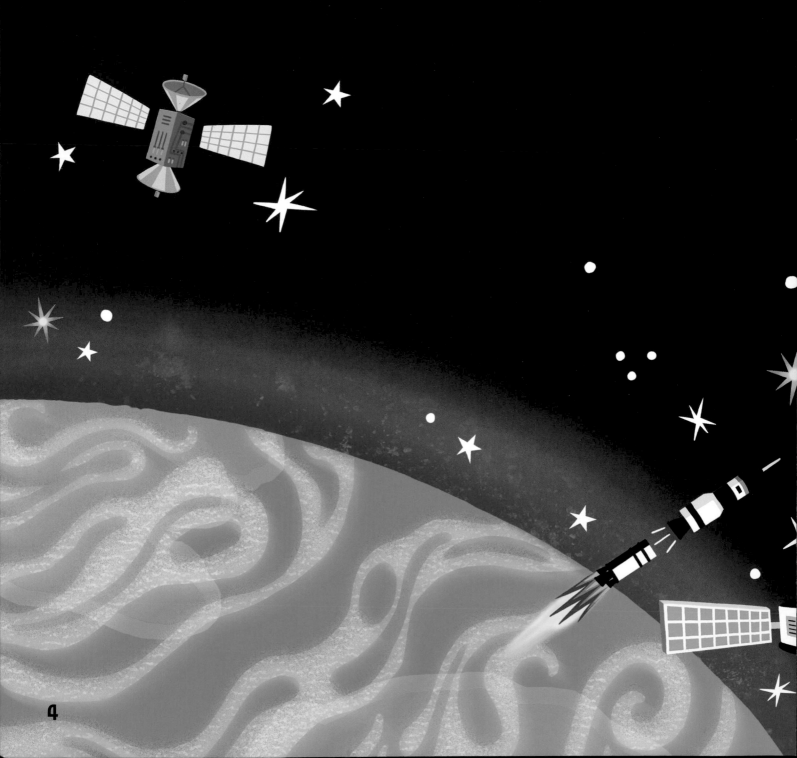

Lift off!

When a rocket launches into the sky, lots of space experts on the ground help everything go to plan. Add people, screens and the rocket... then it's 3-2-1... Lift off!

On the Moon

A few rockets have gone all the way to the Moon, so that astronauts could walk on the dusty, rocky surface. Stick some astronauts onto the picture, then add some space vehicles from the different Moon missions.

Space station

The International Space Station floats high above the Earth, while astronauts do science experiments inside it. Use the stickers to finish building the space station, then add a spacecraft, and some astronauts doing repairs.

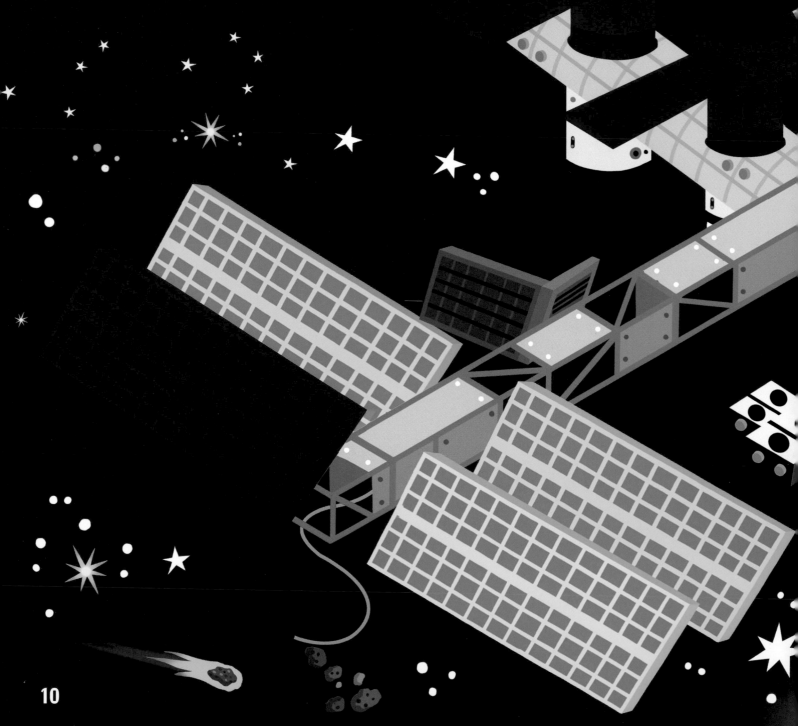

Inside the space station

Life in the space station is complicated because everything floats around when you're in space – including people. Fill the picture with floating astronauts, space food and equipment.

Mars base

One day people hope to travel all the way to the planet Mars, and even to live there. Add buildings, astronauts and vehicles to show how it might look if we travel to Mars in the future.

The night sky

You don't have to be an astronaut to explore space – you can see the stars from the Earth with a telescope. Stick more stars in the night sky, then add some people looking up at them.

Out in space – pages 2-3

Some of the planets have several moons that go around them. Stick the moons on too.

Saturn

Moon of Saturn

Comets (chunks of ice and rock)

Venus

Neptune

Moon of Saturn

Moon of Saturn

Space probe

Uranus

Earth's Moon

Mercury

Mars

Earth

Jupiter

Space probe

Asteroids (huge rocks that hurtle through space)

Moon of Jupiter

Moons of Jupiter

Tourist spaceplane (near future)

Dragon spacecraft (2010)

Hubble Space Telescope (1990)

Space shuttle (1981)

Vostok 1 (1961)

Soyuz TMA spacecraft (2003)

Sputnik 1 (1957)

Apollo 11 spacecraft (1969)

V-2 rocket (1942)

Lift off! - pages 6-7

Control panels

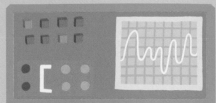

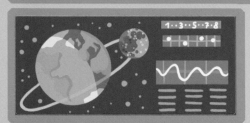

Data screens

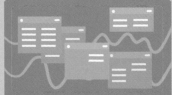

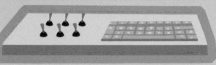

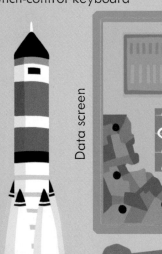

Launch-control keyboard

Launch-control keyboard

Launch-control telephone

Space rocket

Data screen

Chief Engineer

Stick these two people onto the picture last.

Head of Launch Operations

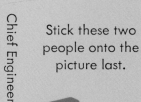

On the Moon - pages 8-9

Command module

Lunar satellite

Footprints

Moon buggy antenna

Lunar satellite

Command module

Moon buggy

Lunar satellite

Collected Moon rocks

Surface crater

Top of landing module

Space station - pages 10-11

Space station module

Solar panel

Section of frame

Recently launched rocket

Station window

Laboratory modules

Satellite

Solar panel

Solar panels

Docked spacecraft

Inside the space station - pages 12-13

Toothbrush

Communicator

Wrench

Astronaut's helmet

Dial panel

Juice

Astronaut's gloves

Water

Fork

Laptop

Laptop

Pliers

Spoon

Station manual

Space pen

Clipboard

Space food

Mars base - pages 14-15

Greenhouse

Roof dish

radio mast

Mars buggies

Greenhouse

Main greenhouse

Communications dish

Living quarters

Walkie-talkies

Mars rover

Control room

Mars surface vehicle

Greenhouse

The Moon

Shooting star

Shooting star

Comet

Open observatory roof

Maps of the Moon

Telescope

Star charts

Laptop

Telescope

Binoculars

Books on space

Telescope